MW01287051

Non–Sequitur

Non–Sequitur
© 2015 Khadijah Queen
All rights reserved.

ISBN: 978-1-933959-29-0

Cover design and typesetting: Mark Addison Smith
Inside image: Ashley Lamb, *Bob and Natalie*, 7x9-inches, collage, 2015

Litmus Press is a program of Ether Sea Projects, Inc., a 501(c)(3)
non-profit literature and arts organization. Dedicated to supporting
innovative, cross-genre writing, the press publishes the work of
translators, poets, and other writers, and organizes public events in
their support. We encourage interaction between poets and visual
artists by featuring contemporary artworks on the covers of our books.
By actualizing the potential linguistic, cultural, and political benefits
of international literary exchange, we aim to ensure that our poetic
communities remain open-minded and vital.

Litmus Press publications are made possible by the New York State
Council on the Arts with the support of Governor Andrew Cuomo
and the New York State Legislature. Additional support for Litmus
Press comes from the Leslie Scalapino–O Books Fund, individual
members and donors. All contributions are fully tax-deductible.

State of the Arts

NYSCA

Litmus Press
925 Bergen Street #405
Brooklyn, New York 11238
litmuspress.org

Small Press Distribution
1341 Seventh Street
Berkeley, California 94710
spdbooks.org

Library of Congress Cataloging-in-Publication Data
Queen, Khadijah.
  Non-sequitur : (a disjointed chorus) / by Khadijah Queen
     pages cm
  ISBN 978-1-933959-29-0
  I. Title.
  PS3617.U443N66 2015
  811'.6--dc23
  2015031257

Khadijah Queen

Non–
Sequitur

(a disjointed chorus)

SETTING

A shifting landscape and evolving interiors anywhere on Earth.

TIME

The present moment.

Non-Sequitur concerns a large group of abstract/ conceptual characters and objects carrying on apparently unrelated conversations and making various observations about the larger world. Their movements and commentary represent an intuited understanding of reality—one that often does not reveal itself in public, out loud, or even to the conscious self—mimicking the chaos of everyday existence. As a subtext, the play explores the relationship between body and text/speech, how the body mediates thought, feeling and perception, enacting unconscious drives and performing/interacting with stereotypes in absurd, unexpected ways.

CONTENTS

Non-Sequitur (a disjointed chorus)

CHARACTERS

Loose Note: A maximum of ten players play multiple roles. Race, age, gender and other appearance markers may vary with individual productions at the discretion of director and playwright, and according to resources.

THE ONLINE PAYMENTS
THE BLONDE INSTITUTION
THE BROWN VAGINA
THE FONDLED HAIR

THE GHOST OF AUDUBON
THE OUTRAGED EXAGGERATOR
THE EXULTANT EXOTIFIER
THE HABITUAL JUSTIFIER

THE CHAKRA BALANCER
THE JESUS FREAKER
THE BREAST CUPPER

THE DIRTY RAG
THE CHARLIE HORSE OPTIMIST
THE HOPED-FOR AFTERMATH
THE ABJECT COMMUNIONIST
THE HALF-OPEN WINDOW

THE MILD EX-PRISONER
THE KILLED ROACH
THE SHRINKING ELITIST

THE MATHEMATICIAN
THE SHIT TALKER
THE ROCK KICKER
THE VOICE OF MALCOLM X

THE READYMADE BRIDE
THE 40% DISCOUNT
THE PREHEATED OVEN

THE WEEKEND YOGA CLASS
THE 15-MINUTE MEDITATION
THE MISSED SLEEP

THE CHRONIC ACCOMPANIER
THE BUDDING WIFE
THE MORNING STUBBLE
THE HAND-ME-DOWN PINKING SHEARS

THE CHIP OFF THE OLD BLOCK
THE EVENT CALENDAR
THE BENT BUSINESS CARD
THE LOST SKETCHBOOK

THE FRAZZLED EVALUATOR
THE MISSPELLED WORDS
THE SIX-MONTH WAIT FOR AN APPOINTMENT

PROLOGUE

(A drummer downstage center playing random rhythms on a djembe, a shirtless white man playing the flute, a ballet dancer in a pink tutu, or a woman on her knees scrubbing the floor.)

ACT I: The Setup

SCENE 1

(PLAYERS enter from the left and line up, evenly spaced, downstage center. Each player is engulfed in a spotlight.)

THE BROWN VAGINA
> I am still not female.

THE BLONDE INSTITUTION
> I can never be invisible.

THE ONLINE PAYMENTS
> Your payment was rejected.

THE FONDLED HAIR
> No.

THE WHITE APPROPRIATION *(moves slightly into shadow)*

THE BROWN VAGINA
> I am an animal to you.

THE BLONDE INSTITUTION
> I can sense your violent thoughts.

THE ONLINE PAYMENTS
> Your payment is past due.

THE FONDLED HAIR *(laughing)*
> No.

THE WHITE APPROPRIATION *(takes a little black notebook from his pocket and begins to write)*

THE BROWN VAGINA
> I am bleeding tonight.

THE BLONDE INSTITUTION
> I feel afraid that something will happen to me.

THE ONLINE PAYMENTS
> Your payment was not input correctly.

THE FONDLED HAIR
> My mother said you can touch her hair.

THE WHITE APPROPRIATION *(begins counting on fingers)*

THE BROWN VAGINA
> I am still giving birth.

THE BLONDE INSTITUTION
> I should have dyed my hair.

THE ONLINE PAYMENTS
> Your payment was less than the minimum.

THE FONDLED HAIR
> No, really. She did!

THE WHITE APPROPRIATION *(licks fingers, touches self)*

> *(The other* PLAYERS *stand and look at audience while he does that for a few moments. Then lights go out,* PLAYERS *exeunt.)*

SCENE 2

(Four spotlights come on. PLAYERS *enter downstage right and line up evenly upstage.* THE OUTRAGED EXAGGERATOR *holds a white plate.)*

THE GHOST OF AUDUBON *(pulls a dirt-encrusted worm from a brown paper bag, places on* OUTRAGED EXAGGERATOR's *plate)*
How about a nice fat worm?

THE OUTRAGED EXAGGERATOR
Yecchhh!!! Who ordered this? I didn't ask for this shit.

THE EXULTANT EXOTIFIER
Oh, just LOOK at her hair ...

THE HABITUAL JUSTIFIER
Why can't we all just get along?

THE GHOST OF AUDUBON *(looks at* OUTRAGED *with pride)*
Your feathers are particularly iridescent this morning.

THE OUTRAGED EXAGGERATOR *(smashes plate on the ground)*
That waiter ain't gettin' no muthafuckin' tip from me!

THE HABITUAL JUSTIFIER
Don't you know the subtext for everything is Harry Potter?

THE EXULTANT EXOTIFIER *(reaches out, longingly, toward imagined subject)*
Oh, her hair is AMAZING, I just HAVE to touch it!

THE GHOST OF AUDUBON
> Would you like a cracker?

> *(Lights go out and* PLAYERS *exeunt, except* GHOST OF AUDUBON—*lights fade as he holds out his hand.)*

SCENE 3

(Three spotlights come on. PLAYERS *enter from downstage right and line up, evenly spaced, downstage center.)*

THE CHAKRA BALANCER *(sits cross-legged in meditation posture, takes several deep breaths)*
Transcend feet and your race will fall off.

THE JESUS FREAKER *(jumping up and down)*
I know that I know that I know that I know!

THE BREAST CUPPER *(looks at hands, makes gesture to cup breasts)*
My hands barely fit around them. *(gets angry)*
Somebody get me a boob sling!

(BLACKOUT)

SCENE 4

(Black & white VIDEO of three pairs of feet at a shore projected on a screen. Stage is dark. VOICES heard offstage.)

THE ABJECT COMMUNIONIST
> I take the body.

THE HALF-OPEN WINDOW
> Rain warped the sill. He's leaning on me.

THE DIRTY RAG
> I think I'll dip my toe into an ocean and call it a swim.

THE CHARLIE HORSE OPTIMIST
> We can start with non-dismissal.

THE HOPED-FOR AFTERMATH
> Please, try to stifle your incredulous guffaws.

THE ABJECT COMMUNIONIST
> I take the blood.

THE HALF-OPEN WINDOW
> I think I need some air.

THE DIRTY RAG
> Nasty ass people.

THE CHARLIE HORSE OPTIMIST
> Maybe the timing isn't right.

THE HOPED-FOR AFTERMATH
> You are more racist than you think you are.

THE HALF-OPEN WINDOW
> Aaahhhhh …

(Projection disappears as lights come on to reveal three bodies behind a screen as shadows)

THE ABJECT COMMUNIONIST *(kneels in prayer)*
> I take yours too.

THE DIRTY RAG *(hands on hips)*
> Tired of soaking up your slop.

THE CHARLIE HORSE OPTIMIST *(grunts, bends over, holding stomach as if punched)*

THE HOPED-FOR AFTERMATH *(picking and biting fingernails)*

> *(BLACKOUT)*

ACT II: Internalizing externalities and vice versa

SCENE 1

> SETTING: A desert. Lights are red. Fierce wind
> sounds play. A black & white video of feathers falling
> is projected on a large screen off center, like a square
> of burned out sun.
>
> *(Three spotlights come on.* PLAYERS *enter from
> right and line up evenly spaced downstage center into
> the spotlights.)*

THE MILD EX-PRISONER
> I didn't sleep well last night.

THE KILLED ROACH *(rubbing stomach, picking teeth)*
> Yeah, I've crawled across many a pillow in my day.

THE SHRINKING ELITIST
> My grandmother would call us a bunch of wild
> Indians if we acted like that.

THE MILD EX-PRISONER *(sighs)*
> I didn't eat very well either.

THE KILLED ROACH
> Took a dump in 1,000 breadboxes.

THE SHRINKING ELITIST
> Do you mind if I take a shower first?

THE KILLED ROACH
> Now *(sighs slowly, dejectedly)* I'm dead.

THE SHRINKING ELITIST
> You've got to call the front office if you need help.

THE MILD EX-PRISONER
The man on top of me snores all night.

(PLAYERS *exeunt.*)

INTERLUDE

*(VIDEO of thighs opening and closing projected on screen.
VOICES heard offstage, speaking slowly.)*

THE SHOE FETISHIST
I might make beauty behave as a whip.

THE SOBER CONSERVATIONIST
Intelligence is a kind of violence.

(Pause for imagined effect.)

SCENE 2

> SETTING: A dinner party. Each player has a wine glass or champagne flute. Various snacks on the table.
>
> (PLAYERS *enter from downstage right and line up in a loose circle center stage.*)

THE ROCK KICKER (*singing Faith Evans mournfully, rocking to imagined beat*)
> You used to love me every day, hmmm-hmmm love has gone away …

THE SHIT TALKER (*smoking hookah*)
> Congratulations! You didn't slap the person who told you that shit.

THE MATHEMATICIAN
> It's a microbe trick. I made up an equation.

THE ROCK KICKER
> Can't you hear me … hmmm-hmmm-hmmm … not what love's about …

THE SHIT TALKER
> Oranges don't come from apple trees.

THE MATHEMATICIAN (*takes off glasses, cleans them slowly with a soft cloth*)

THE ROCK KICKER
> You let me walk around … hmmm-hmmm … it's all right … to let me down—
> (*Pause for a choir of pre-rehearsed members of audience to sing the refrain: "I remember / the way / you used / to love / me".*)

THE SHIT TALKER
>   Amen! Praise Barack!
>
>   *(Several pre-rehearsed members of the audience also shout, "Praise him!")*

THE MATHEMATICIAN *(takes out a huge calculator, starts furiously making calculations)*

>   *(Lights fade,* PLAYERS *exeunt.)*

SCENE 3

(Four spotlights come on. PLAYERS *enter spotlights from downstage right and line up, evenly spaced, center stage.)*

THE VOICE OF MALCOLM X *(offstage recording plays)*
> I said he loved the master better than he loved himself!

THE INVISIBLE INSTITUTION
> Playing with children, playing with adults—same thing.

THE BROWN VAGINA *(points to a door)*
> Somebody left the door open—

THE ONLINE PAYMENTS
> Reminder: please send payment by the due date.

THE VOICE OF MALCOLM X
> My original name was taken from me when my ancestors were brought over in chains.

THE INVISIBLE INSTITUTION *(in a baby voice)*
> Oh. Look at all the misdemeanor contraventions. How cute!

THE BROWN VAGINA
> Yes, I know you'd like me better pinked.

THE ONLINE PAYMENTS
> We have the right to file a judgment against you.

THE INVISIBLE INSTITUTION
> I love my assumptions. They make other people think I'm *(uses air quotes)* "down" with them.

THE VOICE OF MALCOLM X
> Power never takes a back step—only in the face of more power.

THE BROWN VAGINA
>
> I really don't appreciate your microaggressions.

(A chorus of 10 people dressed like ONLINE PAYMENTS *enter from upstage left and line up pyramid style behind him / her. All spotlights shift to them.)*

THE ONLINE PAYMENTS
>
> I'm sorry. Your payment did not go through. Please try again later.

(Lights fade, PLAYERS *exeunt.)*

SCENE 4

SETTING: Projection of a meadow of poppies, a strip mall or a half-empty restaurant meat freezer, all meat freezer-burned.

(PLAYERS *are already onstage, each engulfed in a spotlight that fades in as projection shrinks.*)

THE READYMADE BRIDE *(frowning, bending over and walking around as if looking for something)*
Where's the kitty? Kiiiiiiittttyyyyyyy!

THE PREHEATED OVEN
I'm never empty for long.

THE 40% DISCOUNT *(mopey-faced)*
I'm messed up. Or I messed up.

THE PREHEATED OVEN *(picking at fingernails)*
Don't these people believe in cleaning?

THE 40% DISCOUNT *(looks at outfit, smoothes fabric)*
Then again…

THE READYMADE BRIDE *(stomps foot)*
I can't get married without the kitty!

THE PREHEATED OVEN
I could have sworn I was hot enough already.

THE 40% DISCOUNT *(sighs)*
There isn't enough money in the world.

THE READYMADE BRIDE *(runs offstage, sobbing)*

(*Lights fade,* PLAYERS *exeunt.*)

ACT III: Navigating the spaces

SCENE 1

> SETTING: A room. Lights like a flickering TV: a
> small square of static projected on back wall. YOGA
> CLASS members each have electric blue mats and are
> wearing gray foldover yoga pants. Their tops are a
> mishmash of color.
>
> *(Lights come up on* PLAYERS *already onstage. YOGA
> CLASS made up of three to seven people is centerstage,*
> SLEEP *is downstage right.* MEDITATION *is downstage left,
> each engulfed in a spotlight.)*

THE WEEKEND YOGA CLASS *(a number of people move through five
asanas together: cat pose, child's pose, downward facing dog, plank
pose, warrior posture and repeat)*

THE 15-MINUTE MEDITATION *(in half-lotus position, hands at namaste)*
> Let's settle the inward gaze.

THE MISSED SLEEP *(pimp-walks downstage left, whispers conspiratorially
to audience)*
> I bet this is the movie where enchanted girls do kung fu.

THE WEEKEND YOGA CLASS *(lie on their backs with heads pointed
toward one another and make cycling motions forward then reverse,
speeding up)*

THE 15-MINUTE MEDITATION *(closes eyes and takes deep breaths)*

THE MISSED SLEEP
> I know you're sorry now!

THE 15-MINUTE MEDITATION *(opens eyes, speaks softly but firmly)*
> I can tell when you're doing it for the wrong reasons.

THE WEEKEND YOGA CLASS *(forms a circle, their heads pointed at one another; then begin half-candle pose)*

THE MISSED SLEEP *(pirouettes clumsily at first, then expertly as lights converge upon him or her; other players exeunt when light leaves them. dance completed,* SLEEP *remains in an artful pose, breathing heavily)*

(Lights fade, PLAYERS *exeunt.)*

SCENE 2

> (PLAYERS *enter spotlights from downstage right and line up,*
> *evenly spaced, center stage.* THE CHRONIC ACCOMPANIER
> *sings all lines in varying modes—operatic, R&B, pop, etc.)*

THE HAND-ME-DOWN PINKING SHEARS *(grabs crotch, bites lip, glares*
menacingly)
> Yeah, I cut it. What?

THE MORNING STUBBLE
> Can't get rid of me so easily.

THE CHRONIC ACCOMPANIER
> I've run afoul of my sense of entitlement.

THE BUDDING WIFE *(ties on an apron that says My Milkshake*
Tastes Better Than Yours, smoothes hair)

THE HAND-ME-DOWN PINKING SHEARS
> No one cares if you're struggling.

THE MORNING STUBBLE *(knowingly)*
> At the last minute, we always want to say no.

THE CHRONIC ACCOMPANIER
> In my first year, I wrote a crown of sonnets.

THE BUDDING WIFE *(unsure of where the broom is, looks around*
frantically)

THE HAND-ME-DOWN PINKING SHEARS
> And they don't want to see it happening, either.

THE MORNING STUBBLE
> Humph. Can't get rid of me so easily.

THE CHRONIC ACCOMPANIER
> In my second year, I wrote a one-act play …

THE BUDDING WIFE *(opens mouth to speak, but falls silent)*

THE HAND-ME-DOWN PINKING SHEARS
> This ain't no democracy.

THE MORNING STUBBLE
> My roots go deep.

THE CHRONIC ACCOMPANIER
> In my third year, I wrote fire arias …

THE BUDDING WIFE *(sees the broom upstage, runs toward it)*

THE HAND-ME-DOWN PINKING SHEARS
> What do you think you can do with me that hasn't already been done?

THE MORNING STUBBLE *(snootily)*
> And who wouldn't want whiskers?

THE CHRONIC ACCOMPANIER
> In my fourth year, I wrote a miniature blues libretto …

THE BUDDING WIFE *(begins to sweep)*

THE HAND-ME-DOWN PINKING SHEARS *(opens and closes legs repeatedly, violently, loud snipping sounds heard)*

THE MORNING STUBBLE *(scoffs)*
> Shaving. Act like a toxin is being released.

THE CHRONIC ACCOMPANIER *(in a straight voice, not singing this time)*
> But I'm not here to entertain you.

THE BUDDING WIFE *(drops broom, runs toward the audience screaming)*

(BLACKOUT, PLAYERS *exeunt.)*

SCENE 3

> SETTING: A bedroom. PLAYERS lie in an oversized bed
> onstage. There is a lamp on a nightstand on THE LOST
> SKETCHBOOK's side. The comforter is pastel, lots of
> pillows. A drum beats softly.

THE LOST SKETCHBOOK *(indignantly)*
> Yes, I am from Mississippi.

THE BENT BUSINESS CARD
> There's a best friend for everyone.

THE CHIP OFF THE OLD BLOCK *(reaches behind his/her back, looks at
palm, which is bloody, then looks at audience)*
> I think you just ripped out my asshole.

THE EVENT CALENDAR *(exasperated)*
> You cannot plan this meeting around the season
> premiere of Entourage!

THE CHIP OFF THE OLD BLOCK *(wiping hands on chest)*
> What I'd really like is to be cured, once and for all,
> of Obama Derangement Syndrome.

THE BENT BUSINESS CARD
> There's a diorama for you.

THE LOST SKETCHBOOK *(brings hands to head)*
> I'm having separation anxiety.

THE EVENT CALENDAR
> No tiptoeing allowed!

THE LOST SKETCHBOOK *(staring at CHIP OFF THE OLD BLOCK)*
> That barbecue you're eating?

THE BENT BUSINESS CARD
>That's what the agent said.

THE EVENT CALENDAR
>Well, your food poisoning threw off the whole
>fucking schedule.

THE CHIP OFF THE OLD BLOCK *(smiles brightly, smoking a cigarette)*

>*(BLACKOUT)*

SCENE 4

> SETTING: An office with three cubicles facing the audience. THE FRAZZLED EVALUATOR types the entire time.

THE SIX-MONTH WAIT FOR AN APPOINTMENT
> You have to wait like everyone else.

THE FRAZZLED EVALUATOR
> We must answer all the questions!

THE MISSPELLED WORDS
> It was not wrong!

THE SIX-MONTH WAIT FOR AN APPOINTMENT *(conspiratorially to the audience)*
> Between you and me, if somebody gets too close, I even growl a little bit. GRRRRR …

THE FRAZZLED EVALUATOR
> We don't share that information.

THE MISSPELLED WORDS
> I was almost there, and then everything went white.

THE SIX-MONTH WAIT FOR AN APPOINTMENT
> Waaaahaha!!!! Woohoooohooohoo!!!!! Waahahahahaha!!!!!

THE MISSPELLED WORDS
> C----H----A----R, chair.

THE FRAZZLED EVALUATOR *(stops typing, looks at shirt then at audience)*
> I think I popped a button.

> *(BLACKOUT)*

EPILOGUE

(Sound of scrubbing on the floor. All PLAYERS *come
in on hands and knees with scrub brushes & wearing
white coveralls. Choreographed movements continue
for a full two minutes. One of them draws a chalk circle
around herself, then stands and begins to cry. Another
begins to wail. Everyone else listens, reverently. Yet
another: starts dancing.)*

(CURTAIN)

NOTES

ACT I: SCENE 1
The first line spoken and character name THE BROWN VAGINA, as well as some lines spoken by THE SHIT TALKER, are modified from conversations with Natasha M. Marin.

ACT I: SCENE 2
The Harry Potter line is from a conversation with ariel robello.

ACT I: SCENE 3
The line spoken by THE CHAKRA BALANCER is advice from Thomas Sayers Ellis, when asked how to address the issue of admonishments by a visual art professor to strive for racial transcendence in art.

ACT II: SCENE 3
Lines spoken by THE VOICE OF MALCOLM X are taken from various famous speeches and interviews given by Malcolm X (also known as El Hajj Malik El-Shabazz).

THE DREAM ACT, SCENE 2 *(in Bonus Material)*
Character name and lines spoken by THE ANGEL OF CORN are from a conversation with ariel robello.

AUTHOR'S STATEMENT

I wrote *Non-Sequitur* while thinking about how being African-American (both in America and abroad) often demands a certain degree of performativity. Sometimes one's safety is at stake; other times one's livelihood. Cultural assumptions and social expectations for most people in general can create situations that require intellectual, physical, and psychological acrobatics, but not everyone's survival depends on it. The absurdity, violence, and difficulty of such performance, particularly with regard to the experience I can speak to as a heterosexual Black woman, is both laughable and uncomfortable, and the stage play format encourages more awareness of (unconscious or conscious) participatory roles we all may take on in our own lives in order to perhaps incite both empathy and an acute awareness of the fallout of such participation.

Looking at Act II in particular, conscious and subconscious acts can be discerned via setting and dialogue: amid the wildness of a desert in Scene 1, a dinner party in Scene 2, the stage itself in scene 3, a meadow is interchangeable with a meat freezer or a strip mall in scene 4, and a sensual video during the interlude. The juxtapositions of violence and beauty, the natural world and the contrived world, all stand in for thought. How often do we replay images in our minds, how often do we hear the voices of others as background to thought and memory, affecting choices we make in the present? We bring to any environment our full selves including those thoughts, memories, pasts, bodies, scars, hopes.

The multitude of characters in the play hints at the seeming infinitude of players in our lives, and the sometimes absurd, sometimes abject process of sifting through such influence. Since most of them do not interact with one another, the audience doesn't get drawn into fictive action. Rather, they are asked to create or co-construct with the text a possible container for these scenes and acts and words within which an understanding about the said infinitude of pronouncements and behaviors can be examined on the viewer's or reader's terms.

By incorporating a fragmentary poetics into a dramatic structure, my hope is to have pointed out and challenged ways of seeing that defer to the obvious, and to have expanded ways of seeing into the underside of what's said and done in the play, privileging the unsaid, inspiring discomfort by clearly marking with language and humor the outrageous absurdity of often very painful cultural norms and practices.

Production Note: The following bonus material can be used with the original play or on its own. The deleted scenes can be used in any order and do not all have to be used in production. *The Dream Act* should, however, be performed in its entirety as a standalone or as a prologue or epilogue to *Non-Sequitur*. I kept them out of the play at large to avoid a sense of overwhelm within the repetitiveness, even as it varies so wildly. But, I included the deleted scenes, characters and *The Dream Act* to highlight the infinitude of both absurdity and possibility. As THE SOCIAL DISSERTATIONIST says, I could go on forever.

DELETED CHARACTERS

THE POPULARITY CONTEST
THE HECTIC TED TALK
THE BLACK FARMERS
THE FALSE CHANTERELLE
THE RUINED CROPS
THE BUTTERCUP ANARCHIST
THE CONTINUOUS NON-INDICTMENT
THE CAGEY VETERAN
THE IRONIC ABSOLUTISM
THE POST TRAUMATIC PATRIOT
THE SENIOR HOUSING COMPLEX
THE JAUNTY HUMIDIFIER
THE DOOR CRASHING DEER
THE PREGNANT MUD WRESTLER
THE OVERDONE GEL MANICURE
THE STYLISH COUCH COVER
THE ANONYMOUS COSPLAYER
THE CAREFUL OBSESSION
THE TEXTURED PAINTING
THE PRESSED HAIR
THE WILTED FLORAL ARRANGEMENT
THE LIMP KALE
THE SLAYED STANS
THE OCD COKEHEAD
THE PERFECT DATING PROFILE
THE SUPER LONG WIFI PASSWORD
THE FROG-THROATED BOOTLEGGER
THE BUMPED UP BONUS
THE BORROWED VACUUM
THE IMAGINARY TIME WARP
THE MEMORY OF ASSASSINATION
THE WANNABE IP MAN
THE DILAPIDATED COLONIAL
THE WINK TO ELIOT
THE KIERA KNIGHTLEY HATER

THE TRANSLATED SPECTACLE
THE ENDLESS MONOPOLY GAME
THE FAIR WARNING
THE FLAT EARTH THEORY
THE RESIDENT PARKING
THE INDIVIDUAL EDUCATION PLAN
THE FARTHING FLINGER
THE MOODY CIRCLE K CASHIER
THE MARVELOUS DOGSITTER
THE CLANDESTINE TECHNICIAN
THE 4-IN-1 BUNDLE
THE BOSSY TODDLER
THE LOOP-DE-LOOP PANCAKE FLIPPER
THE BLANK ANALOGY
THE SHO YOU RIGHT
THE SHUT-IN AMUSANT
THE CONVULSIVE FRAILTY
THE FIFTIETH MUSE
THE KLUTZY WUNDERKIND
THE MINT JULEP
THE BURNT BISCUIT
THE KHAKI SHORTS
THE SLAPHAPPY CENTURION
THE MODERN CHANGELING
THE FROWSY ASSISTANT
THE PERMISSIVE GALAXY
THE PAUSED GENERATION
THE FAILED ITERATION
THE SHIT SHOW
THE FORMULAIC CHASE SCENE
THE BAG OF NASTY CAT TREATS
THE ILL-FREQUENTED BISTRO
THE POPULAR SANDBOX
THE TEPID SWAMP
THE WATERY EYE OF A STRANGER
THE SARTRE APOLOGIST
THE CORNERED LILAC

THE BLINGED-OUT TRANSPARENCY
THE THEORETICAL UPHEAVAL
THE IMPOTENT MANIFESTO
THE MARTINET LOUNGE SINGER
THE NEGLECTED SUBLIME
THE LAST THIN MINT
THE TWICE-THRIFTED SOFA BED
THE SINGLE ADIRONDACK CHAIR IN WINTER

DELETED SCENES

MEDICAL INTERLUDE

(Garish lights flash on and off. Cheesy game show or elevator music, or any kind of annoying phone reminder sound, plays. THE HALF-EMPTY PILL BOTTLE *and* THE IPHONE 4 *dance onto the stage from opposite sides, grinning.* IPHONE 4 *can do whatever kind of dance they want: tap, butoh, modern, hip-hop, ballet, jazz, etc.* THE HALF-EMPTY PILL BOTTLE *should do something stilted, robotic or traditional.)*

THE IPHONE 4

Take yo' Celebrex-brex, take yo' Celebrex! *(repeats continuously, while dancing)*

THE HALF-EMPTY PILL BOTTLE *(when center stage, stops dancing, unrolls a scroll, puts on glasses, clears throat and reads the instructions for and side effects of Celebrex printed off the Internet)*

(BLACKOUT)

SCENE i

SETTING: A late-night dinner party in the middle of
a desert. The table is covered in random objects and
photographs of food. The guests sit on large white
plates and wear wine glasses strapped onto their heads.
In this scene, PLAYERS can be the same, with lights
fading out and a slight adjustment in wardrobe taking
place. Or the table can seat all characters but only the
relevant ones speak while others remain silent and still
as statues. THE GRACIOUS HOST has a Southern accent.

THE CLANTON PEACH
Love the tumultuous gesture.

THE GRACIOUS HOST *(smiles)*
Someone went to the School of Imagistic Silence.

THE EVERYDAY COOK *(looks all around, under the plates, under the
table, puzzled)*
All the cherries are gone.

THE FALLEN SOUFFLE *(in a floaty voice)*
Atmospheric changes?

THE GRACIOUS HOST
He sings Twinkle, Twinkle Little Star and I just melt.

THE EVERYDAY COOK *(stirring something in a large pot, steam rising)*
Look at this gorgeous color coming from the meat.
Mmmmm … smells so good.

THE CLANTON PEACH *(moans in rapture)*

THE FALLEN SOUFFLE *(in a warning tone)*
That's … too … polite.

THE EVERYDAY COOK *(lifts spoon, some liquid drips from it; looks at audience and offers a crooked smile, as if in apology)*
>It all gets reeeeeeeally soupy at this point.

THE GRACIOUS HOST *(fiddles with necklace, nervously, then looks at each guest as if seeing for the first time)*
>Please. Make yourselves comfortable. Please.

(BLACKOUT)

SCENE ii

> SETTING: A typical cluttered basement laboratory.
> Beakers filled with various colored liquids, some
> steaming. Notebooks strewn about in various states
> of openness. A lab coat tossed onto a backless stool
> at a stainless steel table. Snacks nearby. THE TRIO OF
> BELLY DANCERS enter on relevé and speak together.

THE TRIO OF BELLY DANCERS *(doing candle arms)*
> There's something indecorous about dragging around
> one's wounded body in public.

THE PACKAGE OF GUMMY BEARS *(talking to self, breathing in and out
loudly, hands on hips)*
> Go on. Suck it in.

THE SOFTENED CORNEA *(floating in a jar of clear fluid)*
> Waxy, waxy, waxy stuff.

THE GLISTENING TITLE *(plays with a silicone breast implant)*
> That was *(does a little shimmy, creating a small
> glitter cloud)* desirable.

THE PACKAGE OF GUMMI BEARS *(rubs stomach, tries to suck it in)*

THE TRIO OF BELLY DANCERS *(doing a Turkish drop with snake arms)*
> Bleeding and moaning.

THE SOFTENED CORNEA
> How many months further, watching in vain?

THE GLISTENING TITLE *(stretches the implant)*
> He was *(another glitter shimmy)* into that?

THE PACKAGE OF GUMMY BEARS *(pinches supposed fat rolls)*
> Cake is never a problem.

THE SOFTENED CORNEA *(falls to the bottom)*
>   The image came through in numbers.

THE GLISTENING TITLE
>   I was meant to *(glitter shimmy, shake and pose)* be
>   more than seen.

THE TRIO OF BELLY DANCERS *(spinning around the table)*
>   Look at me, look at me, look!

>   *(BLACKOUT)*

SCENE iii

(Lights fade in, PLAYERS *form a triangle on stage.)*

THE FAILED PROSECUTOR

> I mean, this guy picked up a hooker so he could drive in the carpool lane, got a speeding ticket, and he was still late for the arraignment. Judge threw the book at him.

THE STATED LEARNING DISABILITY

> Memory ain't about to wait.

THE EPONYMOUS FLASH DRIVE

> I feel like saying a Beatnik poem.

THE FAILED PROSECUTOR *(shuffles papers)*

> Not a devastating case, but still...

THE STATED LEARNING DISABILITY

> You stupid fuck!

THE EPONYMOUS FLASH DRIVE *(starts reciting a Beatnik poem, preferably Bob Kaufman's "On")*

THE FAILED PROSECUTOR *(sits down, pounds the stage with fist and shouts three times)*

THE STATED LEARNING DISABILITY *(laughs, sadly, shaking head)*

THE EPONYMOUS FLASH DRIVE

> I woke up to find that I was mourning.

(BLACKOUT)

SCENE iv

> *(Lights fade in,* PLAYERS *already on stage.* THE FUN AND
> GAMES, *two people, stand center stage playing the hand
> game Slide with each other. They alternate parts of the
> lines, one saying the words before the comma, the other
> saying the words after the comma. The others stand
> loosely arranged downstage left.)*

THE FUN AND GAMES

> If you must know, last night I dreamed of baby
> alligators.

THE FLIPPED SWITCH

> I heard you got locked up.

THE SHEER LEGGINGS

> You can still see the skin, right?

THE IMITATION CYCLIST

> You've got to think of it as temporary.

THE FUN AND GAMES

> And the night before that, I was somebody's
> concubine.

THE FLIPPED SWITCH

> Go ahead. Call collect.

THE SHEER LEGGINGS

> Pressed tight against the fabric?

THE IMITATION CYCLIST

> All day, all night, take it all in.

THE FUN AND GAMES

> In other words, a rich and impotent hunter.

THE SHEER LEGGINGS
> After a while there's swelling and something must be removed.

THE FLIPPED SWITCH
> Otherwise ... Zap!!!

THE IMITATION CYCLIST
> Then ride into the veil of light.

THE FUN AND GAMES *(do a final hand clap together, then cross their arms over their chests)*

> *(BLACKOUT)*

MUSICAL INTERLUDE

(A low purple light fades in. Footsteps heard offstage. THE INSTANT MIRACLE *waltzes in with a xylophone, a mandolin, a didgeridoo or any unexpected instrument, but not a harp. Optional effects in the background: smoke machine that comes in at the bridge, a video mashup of oil spill footage, nuclear waste sites and kitten memes, or a 1980s-style text animation of the lyrics, with the n-word and other expletives starred out.)*

THE INSTANT MIRACLE *(Makes a flourish of setting up; straightens cuffs, tie, hat or other elaborate detail; perhaps wearing suspenders and a skirt; finally settles, plays entirety of Tupac Shakur's "Hail Mary" on its instrument, then waltzes back out)*

(Purple lights remain up for next scene.)

SCENE v

> SETTING: A kitchen, wee morning hours.

THE HERNIA, REPAIRED
> There was a hole in me, then another.

THE RECOVERING INSOMNIAC *(puts on water for tea, gets cheese and loaf of bread from fridge)*

THE UNSWEETENED PLANTAINS *(sighs nonchalantly)*
> No one wants me anymore.

THE HERNIA, REPAIRED
> A probing, with something inhuman.

THE RECOVERING INSOMNIAC *(puts two slices of each on a plate, goes back to fridge for mayo)*

THE UNSWEETENED PLANTAINS *(incredulous)*
> No one wants me anymore.

THE HERNIA, REPAIRED
> I had twisted enough that they wanted to straighten me out.

THE UNSWEETENED PLANTAINS *(angry)*
> No one wants me anymore!

THE RECOVERING INSOMNIAC *(makes sandwich, puts on Family Feud on the small kitchen TV, leans over the counter to watch and eat)*

THE HERNIA, REPAIRED
> There was a hole in me, then another.

THE RECOVERING INSOMNIAC *(tea whistles as audience on TV claps and laughs)*

THE UNSWEETENED PLANTAINS *(over the course of days, rots in its Styrofoam box before getting tossed)*

(BLACKOUT)

SCENE vi

> SETTING: Inside multiple social and dating apps on
> a smartphone.

THE HAPPY SINGLE *(on smartphone, singing to the tune of "Reunited"*
by Peaches & Herb, dance-swaying a little)
> Unfriending exes and it feeeeeels so goooooooooood …

THE NOSTRADAMUS PREDICTIONS *(whispering, to audience)*
> Is anyone blood related to a pig yet?

THE ELUSIVE LOVE *(reminds everyone, softly, of their presence)*

THE TINDER NERD *(swiping)*
> I like him, he's an Aquarius.

THE GRINDR ADDICT *(singing to self)*
> I'ma be that noise noise noise noise noise.

THE EHARMONY SKEPTIC
> If someone tries to attack me, I could stab 'em in the
> neck with my pen.

THE HAPPY SINGLE
> Venus is retrograde and they talkin' shiiiiiiiiit …

THE NOSTRADAMUS PREDICTIONS
> Sometimes my timing's a little off, but cut me some
> freakin' slack.

THE TINDER NERD
> I bet they used electromagnetic waves back in the
> 1940s.

THE GRINDR ADDICT *(starts taking lewd selfies)*

THE EHARMONY SKEPTIC *(typing)*
> Can I be frank, or are you the type who likes to
> think women shit roses and rainbows?

THE IN-APP PURCHASER
> Ooh, sparkly roses! I'm buying that.

THE HAPPY SINGLE
> It's kinda funny cuz they're so full of iiiiiiiiiit …

THE ELUSIVE LOVE *(gets loved, then rejects it)*

THE TINDER NERD *(starts taking bathroom selfies, with duckface)*

THE NOSTRADAMUS PREDICTIONS
> And just remember I told you about those daytime
> eruptions.

THE EHARMONY SKEPTIC *(starts taking pretentious selfies with a
selfie stick)*

THE IN-APP PURCHASER (squeals with glee)
> Ooh, yesssss, rainbows! I'm buying those, too.

THE ELUSIVE LOVE *(wears rainbows, leaps about like Legolas
from "Lord of the Rings")*

THE HAPPY SINGLE *(really in jam mode now)*
> I'm so ex-cited cuz I … ain't a-bout it, hey
> heeeeyyyyyy!

> *(BLACKOUT)*

SCENE vii

> SETTING: Video, split screen. Side A: standard
> bathroom, very beige, meticulously clean, with THE
> INTERNAL MONOLOGUE. Side B: park bench, close to
> sunset, with THE EMO REVOLUTIONARY.

THE INTERNAL MONOLOGUE *(wets face, exfoliates, moisturizes, pats
dry, leans on sink, looks in mirror, sighs with irritation, speaks
slowly and with varied emotion)*

> What if I stopped caring what I look like?
> What if I could trust? What if I tried to love
> someone without running?

THE EMO REVOLUTIONARY *(sniffs, checks pockets, looks around)*

> I need some tissue up in this piece …

THE INTERNAL MONOLOGUE *(puts up post-its on mirror)*

> What if I finished that novel and wrote another
> and another? What if I ate less junk?
> What if I slept all night instead of crying?
> What if my tears were a nightmare?

THE EMO REVOLUTIONARY *(deep sigh of annoyance)*

> I need some BLACK tissue up in this piece!

THE INTERNAL MONOLOGUE *(puts up post-its on mirror)*

> What if I expected the best?
> What if I forgive myself for everything?

THE EMO REVOLUTIONARY *(a policeman walks by;* EMO *stiffens, but
doesn't move; officer takes a long look but doesn't speak; keeps
walking;* EMO *watches leaves fall, and sighs)*

> It's almost autumn.

THE INTERNAL MONOLOGUE

> What if I wrote poems during the apocalypse!

THE EMO REVOLUTIONARY *(wipes face with both hands)*
> I can love myself, but is it enough?

THE INTERNAL MONOLOGUE *(with deep sadness, lowers head, then looks at self again)*
> What if I wasn't prone to breaking?

THE EMO REVOLUTIONARY *(phone beeps, checks phone)*
> What in the—*(laughs)* thank Black Jesus for Black Twitter.

THE INTERNAL MONOLOGUE *(after a pause and almost breakdown, changes to a Eureka! face)*
> What if I didn't hold my farts in!

THE EMO REVOLUTIONARY *(phone beeps again, checks phone)*
> Oh shit, it's time for my Shonda shows! *(rushes off)*

THE INTERNAL MONOLOGUE *(smiles, nods, hangs towel, straightens spine)*

> *(BLACKOUT)*

THE DREAM ACT

CHARACTERS

Note: A maximum of four players play multiple roles.
Race, age, gender and other appearance markers may vary
with individual productions at the discretion of director and
playwright, and according to resources.

THE BEL CANTO
THE FAIT ACCOMPLI
POSITIVE POLLY

THE DREAM KILLER
THE ANGEL OF CORN
THE SOCIAL DISSERTATIONIST
THE GOOGLE CHAT STATUS

THE COLORATURA
THE CHAIRMAN OF ENTERTAINMENT
THE DREAM ABOUT MISMATCHED SHOES
THE SALTED CARAMEL MOCHA

SOMNIUM EFFIGY
FLESH EFFIGY

SETTING: For Scenes 1–3, choose one from one or more of the
following: anything from the first act of an Ibsen play, a scene
from the fifth chapter in any Octavia Butler novel, or a simply
a repeating projection of one or all of the following: Graciela
Iturbide photographs, still life images from Neruda's odes, or
the mural of ODB in Brooklyn. For the latter, call the setting
REPEATED PROJECTION and treat it like a static character in all
scenes. Or, let the setting be outer space.

SOUND: "Mass Appeal" by Gang Starr or the instrumental
version of Big Sean's "IDFWU".

SCENE 1

THE BEL CANTO *(slowly, spreading hands and arms open)*
    Welcome, sensitive population …

THE FAIT ACCOMPLI
    Before dawn, the muscles gather to bone and squeeze.
    It feels like all night rabbit punches.

POSITIVE POLLY *(to the audience)*
    Can I tell you something? My physical therapist is
    the BEST.

THE BEL CANTO *(whispers)*
    I have an anxiety disorder. In retrospect, a slow stutter …

THE FAIT ACCOMPLI
    It feels like a wish for paralysis is reasonable. It feels
    extreme, without the pleasure of falling through air,
    the aftermath of landing.

POSITIVE POLLY
    She applies just enough pressure to loosen those traps.

THE BEL CANTO
    And I'm drawing self-portraits in pain, making stump
    rubbings in an arbitrary fortress ruin …

THE FAIT ACCOMPLI
    Weaknesses unearned and unwelcome.

THE BEL CANTO
    I think in triplicate amazement, tough, subtle, estoteric
    debauchery as best mission …

THE FAIT ACCOMPLI
    Small accumulations, the array of attack dull slaps in
    miniature becoming the usual beast

POSITIVE POLLY

> You know what else I love? I love that pressed hair
> smell. Especially when you grease it up first.

THE BEL CANTO

> … all swoon, revoked. *(lowers head, looks at hands)*

THE FAIT ACCOMPLI

> I'd like to astonish you with my language, but only in
> your dreams.

POSITIVE POLLY *(skips offstage)*

> *(BLACKOUT)*

SCENE 2

SOUND: "Give Up" by FKA Twigs

THE DREAM KILLER *(in a bootleg, grayscale Technicolor dreamcoat)*
What kind of idiot pays attention to dreams? How can you even afford that?

THE ANGEL OF CORN *(chewing gum)*
Absurdism is my life. Between the ground of absurd and ism is where I live.

THE SOCIAL DISSERTATIONIST *(smoking a Black & Mild, paces slowly back and forth the whole time but stops abruptly to deliver lines)*
How can people not be into anti-racist dystopian theories?

THE GOOGLE CHAT STATUS *(throughout, takes baby steps in a square on stage, speaking lines when right behind another character, peeking over their shoulder)*
Something's not right.

THE DREAM KILLER *(snorts)*
Also, and I should know, you're terrible at voguing.
(starts voguing, really well actually)

THE ANGEL OF CORN *(clearly high on an illegal substance)*
There's an Aryan in my bed speaking Norwish. I'm going to put something Norwish on my body. I think it makes perfect sense.

THE SOCIAL DISSERTATIONIST
Let me advocate for the devil on this one ... what's really the difference between Miley twerking and my li'l cousin Reggie IV deciding to join the ballet?

THE GOOGLE CHAT STATUS
Trying to reconnect ...

THE DREAM KILLER
> That's hard to believe, given your questionable
> history of sniffing trash.

THE ANGEL OF CORN *(really convinced)*
> In the right context, a tattoo artist would say of course I
> know Norwish. It's better than a tattoo of corn on your
> ass. We could be like Camus and do waiting for Norwish.

THE SOCIAL DISSERTATIONIST *(stops pacing)*
> And also, some days you just don't wanna think about
> how the rape and enslavement of your ancestors
> shows up in your facial structure.

THE ANGEL OF CORN *(looks around, confused, scratches head)*

THE GOOGLE CHAT STATUS
> Whoops …

THE SOCIAL DISSERTATIONIST *(strokes chin)*
> How does one astonish a racist? You would actually
> think it's easy, but *(blows smoke)* not the case. I would
> tell you about that lady who didn't seem to like how I
> spread out my books and laptop at the big table in the
> coffee shop, but if I start listing I could go on forever.

THE ANGEL OF CORN *(frowning, hands on hips)*
> Why is there a didgeridoo in the background?

THE GOOGLE CHAT STATUS
> Try now.

THE DREAM KILLER *(smiles evilly, opens coat like a flasher, brandishing an array of weapons)*

> *(BLACKOUT)*

SCENE 3

> *(Intro sound, fading as players enter from offstage in*
> *ostentatious costumes with great swagger at varied paces:*
> *Mon coeur s'ouvre à ta voix by Jessye Norman. They can*
> *land anywhere on stage and move around or stand at will.)*

THE COLORATURA
>Your own abduction in a dream signifies helplessness.

THE CHAIRMAN OF ENTERTAINMENT
>You can't con a con man, I heard that in a movie.

THE DREAM ABOUT MISMATCHED SHOES *(nodding, excited)*
>In his traveler's mind, the Bulgarians were relevant.

THE SALTED CARAMEL MOCHA *(looking all sexy)*
>It's okay if you fetishize me.

THE COLORATURA
>If you're holding someone else against their will,
>let go.

THE CHAIRMAN OF ENTERTAINMENT
>I don't have any favorites; I like to say I like them all.

THE DREAM ABOUT MISMATCHED SHOES
>He would go from Bulgarians to Papa Smurf.

THE SALTED CARAMEL MOCHA *(continues preening)*
>I'm just the right balance of power and sweetness.

THE COLORATURA
>Nothing there about how feminism enters the collective
>unconscious. But, forgetting to reside in the core of
>grief, you could learn to knit Fair Isle sweaters for
>your captor(s).

THE CHAIRMAN OF ENTERTAINMENT
>But honestly, I haven't been this bored since the early 1990s so I'm drawing a blank.

THE DREAM ABOUT MISMATCHED SHOES
>Now that fool is Googling all 54 countries in Africa! *(walks off hurriedly downstage left, shaking head)*

THE SALTED CARAMEL MOCHA *(posing, downstage right)*
>You know you want me. No whip. *(struts across stage, switching hips, until downstage left exit)*

>*(BLACKOUT)*

SCENE 4

SETTING: A clear day, bright blue sky, few clouds; five crows float to a centerline lamppost on a busy street *(can be a projection)*. Elton John's "Believe" plays. Lights fade in on players center stage an arm's length apart. As one talks, the other rhythmically hums, stomps like Black fraternities/sororities, or does a Riverdance, but not so loudly as to drown out the other character.

SOMNIUM EFFIGY

I had a dream last night parts of my body were not my body, not myself.

My legs went to Harvard. My stretch-marked chest resettled from Iraq. Compton claimed my hands and my shoulders, Cape Cod. I wish I could explain it. But my throat came from the woods of Germany and my mouth spoke only Xhosa.

FLESH EFFIGY

I dreamed I could find a place for all the places my body had been. My Andalusian hips could sit somewhere with ease and softness, like the texture of dyed silk.

My hair lost all its color. My eyes belonged to the owls. I could fill my belly, more French than Italian, with Petit Verdot and dark roux.

Everything I could smell, though, led me to Korean BBQ kitchens, which means I could be a tourist. But I couldn't lift my arms unless I carried wood from the Brazil nut tree, and only then to make fire, not paper.

I didn't feel lost. I felt off-kilter, disconnected, but I knew *(because my brain went back to its beginnings)* that I could make myself whole, somewhere.

SOMNIUM EFFIGY and FLESH EFFIGY *(together, holding hands)*
      And I wake up as the only thing not burning

      (CURTAIN)

Acknowledgements

A shorter version of *Non-Sequitur* appears in *Black Peculiar* (Las Cruces, NM: Noemi Press 2011). Many thanks to Noemi Press publishers Carmen Giménez Smith and Evan Lavender Smith.

The author statement is excerpted from an essay in *Family Resemblance: An Anthology and Exploration of Eight Hybrid Literary Genres* (Chicago, IL: Rose Metal Press 2015). Act II also appears in the anthology.

The list of deleted characters appears in *LitHub* (Fall 2015).

Thank you to ariel robello, Ashaki M. Jackson, Natasha M. Marin, Bettina Judd, Anastacia Tolbert, and Tiffany Anderson for your spectacularly fly friendship, brilliance, and support. Thank you to Red Thread—Susan Southard, Anne Liu Kellor, Anne Canright, and Christin Taylor—for early eyes and encouragement. Deep gratitude to the Leslie Scalapino Award administrators, Fiona Templeton and The Relationship: E. Tracy Grinnell and Litmus Press, Emily Skillings, Alexis Pope: the New Ohio Theater and the cast from the reading on November 14, 2014 and subsequent production (Helga Davis, Whitney V. Hunter, Danielle Davenport, Dawn Saito, Leonora Champagne, Zselyke Tarnai, and David Thompson) for bringing *Non-Sequitur* to life so beautifully and generously.

Non-Sequitur

FIRST PUBLIC READING: at the New Ohio Theatre, New York, November 17, 2014

COMPANY: The Relationship, directed by Fiona Templeton

CAST: Lenora Champagne, Helga Davis, April Matthis, Whitney Hunter, Dawn Saito, Zselyke Tarnai, David Thomson

FIRST PRODUCTION: at Theaterlab, New York, December 10-20, 2015

COMPANY: The Relationship, directed by Fiona Templeton

CAST: Lenora Champagne, Helga Davis, Stacey Robinson, Yon Tande, Dawn Saito, Zselyke Tarnai, David Thomson

COSTUMES: Liz Prince

CHOREOGRAPHIC CONSULTANT: Daria Faïn

LIGHTING: Jeff Nash

The Leslie Scalapino Award production was supported by a grant from the LeslieScalapino/O Books Fund. The Relationship was also funded in part by New York State Council on the Arts. A guest production of Theaterlab.

WWW.THERELATIONSHIP.ORG
WWW.LESLIESCALAPINOAWARD.ORG

green press
INITIATIVE

Litmus Press is committed to preserving ancient forests and
natural resources. We elected to print this title on 30% post
consumer recycled paper, processed chlorine free. As a result, for
this printing, we have saved:

1 Trees (40' tall and 6-8" diameter)
406 Gallons of Wastewater
1 million BTU's of Total Energy
28 Pounds of Solid Waste
75 Pounds of Greenhouse Gases

Litmus Press made this paper choice because our printer,
Thomson-Shore, Inc., is a member of Green Press Initiative, a
nonprofit program dedicated to supporting authors, publishers,
and suppliers in their efforts to reduce their use of fiber obtained
from endangered forests.
For more information, visit www.greenpressinitiative.org.

Environmental impact estimates were made using the Environmental Defense
Paper Calculator. For more information visit: www.papercalculator.org.